The Retreat Story

Restoring Lives

Chad McComas & Staff

Table of Contents

CHAPTER EIGHT

CHAPTER NINE

CHAPTER TEN

CHAPTER ONE

Foreword

Fifty years ago this spring, I rolled into Southern Oregon's Rogue Valley in a beat-up old truck, a love-at-first-sight experience. In the decades since, I've marvelled at how reliably its residents rally together to strengthen the systems that help those in need. Our network of community nonprofits is extraordinary. It's a central reason that this valley of some 300,000 people punches above its weight when it comes to meeting daunting social and economic challenges with effective innovations.

There's one organization that stands out for punching far above its weight. My first taste of what Rogue Retreat had to offer was when founder Chad McComas toured me around Hope Village, then a cluster of 14 shelters, each approximately 8 x 10 feet, just enough space for a bed and chair for an individual or couple coming off the cold streets of Medford. These huts had no plumbing or electricity; the one pre-existing house on the property had been converted to a common area for cooking, eating, bathroom purposes, doing laundry, and just hanging out together sharing games and videos.

Hope Village was a good name. I talked to men and women feeling hopeful for the first time in years after a long stretch of barren and dismal time on the streets. They were daring to dream and set plans for themselves again.

What struck me was how well Rogue Retreat's core strategy fit their aspirations. They aim much higher than triaging the pain of the homeless, merely getting them warm and dry for a few nights at a time (though that's no small thing when you're wet and cold on the Northwest's streets with no place to go).

Rogue Retreat has assembled a continuum of services, beginning with the rudimentary low-barrier shelter of a Hope Village hut, or the larger tent-and-canopy urban campground they've established in Medford, through assisted cooperative living and subsidized housing that nourish skills and responsibility until some of their clients move on to fully independent market-rate housing and lives of productive self-sufficiency.

They're resourceful in finding and deploying a variety of "wrap-around" social services that make durable recovery possible. In the end, they've found a formula for restoring hope not just to the people they serve directly, but to all of us who have sad moments of wondering if we'll ever be able to turn around our spiraling social problems, with houselessness towards the top of the list.

Rogue Retreat doesn't just theorize on the turnaround. Person by person, family by family, they're making it happen.

There's no magic formula for their success. But I think I know the key ingredients: profound compassion, the humility to listen to the people they serve rather than lecture to them, a smart and enterprising staff of continual learners, a fierce commitment to guiding people to more self-sufficient and satisfying lives, and a base of community volunteers who fully share their vision… people with what I've come to see after all these years as a kind of Rogue Valley patriotism.

They bring to mind the legendary Tom McCall, Oregon's sitting governor when I came to the state half a century ago. He's remembered for a lot of salty comments, some of them wise. The one that applies here is that "Heroes are not statues framed against a red sky. They are individuals who say, 'This is my community, and it is my responsibility to make it better.'"

I'm deeply grateful for the heroes of Rogue Retreat.

Oregon State Senator Jeff Golden

Jackson County, Oregon

CHAPTER TWO
Preface

The Rogue Retreat story is literally too good to be true.

Starting in 1998 as the dream of a few caring people who wanted to do something for those in the community who were falling through the cracks to becoming an organization (at this writing) with over 400 homeless individuals a night being served by 100 dedicated employees who see their jobs as more of a ministry to bring hope to the hopeless.

We wanted this book to be an inspiration. Donnie Harper (mentioned later in the book) pushed us to get it written and out to the public. He wanted the story to be told. He wanted others to be inspired, and he knew others were watching.

We get regular requests from other City, County and State officials looking for ideas and programs that work to address the homeless challenges they are facing where they live. The possibility of this book giving hope and creating a spark of creativity to make a difference somewhere is truly our driving force.

We can't take credit for all that has happened. We are not officially a faith-based organization, but we believe there is a power greater than ourselves which has given us more favour than we have deserved to do this work.

You will notice I use the word homeless to identify the population many are beginning to call houseless. I like the word homeless for, as Alan Graham from Mobile Loaves and Fishes in Austin, Texas says: *"Homelessness is caused by a profound catastrophic loss of family."*

When organizations like Rogue Retreat create safe places to be for those with no home, they are inadvertently creating a "family" atmosphere which participants begin to call "home". And this is what they need desperately. Home.

As you read this short book, we hope you get inspired and want to make a difference in your community. And, if we can help, we invite you to reach out to us. Come for a visit. Leave with a dream!

Chapter Three

Introduction

Some stories are hopeful and inspiring! They connect us to what it's like to be human.

Told through the eyes of Chad McComas, Executive Director, and staff of Rogue Retreat, this is one such book, a unique look into the saga of those living on the streets.

The magic of *The Rogue Retreat Story* is that we get a unique glimpse into the transition from hopeless to hopeful.

Tom Fischer, Rogue Retreat Board President and Board Member since 2008, proudly stated to an advisory group recently that *"we (at Rogue Retreat) pride ourselves in meeting people where they're at."*

- What does it mean to reach people experiencing homelessness where they're at?
- What does it mean to be met where they're at?
- Why is this even important in the first place?

This book answers these questions and more.

If you're not familiar with Rogue Retreat, you're in for a treat! On the pages of this book, you will learn about:

- The history of Rogue Retreat (Chapter Four)
- Two success stories of staff – Shannon and Donnie -- with "lived experience" from the streets (Chapter Five)
- Rogue Retreat's "secret sauce," a key to its success (Chapter Six)
- Three transitional housing, shelter and managed campground models (Chapter Seven):
    - Transitional Housing - Hope Village is Southern Oregon's first and model gated tiny house community of 34 units for homeless men, women, and couples.
    - Transitional Shelter - The Kelly Shelter is the first year-round, low barrier (housing first) shelter in Southern Oregon for up to 64 people sheltered per night.
    - Transitional (Managed) Campground - The Medford Urban Campground started with 25 campsites, but has expanded to 70 tent sites (Phase 1) and 25 pallet shelters and 10 tiny houses (Phase 2) with the City of Medford approval.
- Three social enterprises (Chapter Eight):
    - Thrift Shop - The Thrift Shop offers a variety of items at discounted prices for the community. They accept gently-used

donations to resell to the community. All proceeds support the Homeless Supportive Housing/Shelter programs of Rogue Retreat.

o   Clean Sweep - The mission of Clean Sweep by Rogue Retreat is to improve the community's image while providing work opportunities for our homeless volunteers. For a couple of hours of work cleaning the streets, businesses and communities, the homeless volunteers get a $10 gift certificate.

o   Hope University - Hope University, according to Chad, is ultimately "*a way to train and educate other communities. We pat them on the back, pump them up, tell them we made every mistake in the book. Learn from our mistakes so you don't have to make them. They're thrilled.*"

- The expansion plan of "one more bed" (Chapter Nine)
- Four ways to get involved (Chapter Ten)

Since its inception in 1998, there have been many challenges for a fledgling non-profit organization, some of which you will also discover in this book. Leaders within Rogue Retreat and the community have faced these challenges with a profound sense of humility and purpose, fulfilling on a daily basis its mission:

To create opportunities for the homeless to have hope!

"Homelessness is like falling into a well," says Chad McComas, *"it doesn't matter how you get into the well you can't get out without a hand up."*

This is a book of what that "hand up" looks like. It's about regaining some sense of dignity and stability after falling into that well, often without a lifeline of hope or a hand up.

Unlike most books that are written by one or more authors, this book was spoken. Interviews with Chad McComas, Executive Director of Rogue Retreat, and staff were recorded then transcribed by Peter Kimpo. Transcriptions were then edited first by Stephanie Williams from Hot Ghost Writer, then by Phil Johncock, and finally by Chad. The cover was designed by Queen Graphics from Fiverr.

Let's kick off with the History of Rogue Retreat...

CHAPTER FOUR
History of Rogue Retreat

Along the way, Rogue Retreat faced many challenges that revealed its true character in trying to meet unhoused community members where they're at. There were no paid employees until eleven years into its operation. Until that point, everyone was a volunteer.

Volunteers are great and important all the time! Unfortunately, they're not as naturally committed as regular employees. As a result, some things fell apart. Many unintentional mistakes were made.

In addition, it is very unlikely that a truly sustainable non-profit organization can rely solely on volunteers. In fact, without paid staff to operate programs 24 hours per day and being run strictly by volunteers things didn't go well. One result was accruing a financial debt of $40,000.

Even when there seemed to be no hope in sight for the organization's future as a result of getting into debt, the volunteer leadership of Rogue Retreat kept their faith regarding the future of the organization and where it might go.

Executive Director, Chad McComas, is a man of faith. He has been a pastor since 1977. He started out as a volunteer pastor in Corvallis, Oregon, working with students at Oregon State University. He later transferred to a large professional Medford church in 1991. It was on the East side of the city across town from the poor and homeless on the West side of Medford.

According to Chad, the homeless initially "freaked him out." He never would have imagined himself in the position of leading a non-profit serving the homeless, but God had other ideas.

One night in 1997, Chad had a dream that was particularly meaningful and vivid. In this dream, God took him to the streets of Medford on the West side. He was shown people with absolutely no sense of hope or faith. Their eyes were dark and hollow. God turned to Chad and said, *"I want you to set them free."* Chad responded: *"I don't know how."* God said simply, *"I'll show you."*

From that dream, Chad started an organization called Set Free Christian Fellowship. Chad's true desire was to help those who fell between the cracks of society and needed a hand up. He wanted to give these people a sense of hope. Part of the need was services to help the homeless and thus in 1998 Rogue Retreat was born.

The word "rogue" in "Rogue Retreat" carries several related and relevant meanings:

- To "go rogue" means *"to begin to behave in an independent or uncontrolled way that is not authorized, normal, or expected."* (source: Merriam Dictionary)

- "Rogue" may also refer to a *"vagrant"* *("one who has no established residence and wanders idly from place to place without lawful or visible means of support").* (source: Merriam Dictionary)

- "Rogue" colloquially can mean *"untamed, wild and out of control."*

- Rogue Retreat is geographically located in the Rogue Valley, Oregon. According to Wikipedia, *"The Rogue Valley is a valley region in southwestern Oregon… Located along the middle Rogue River and its tributaries in Josephine and Jackson counties, the valley forms the cultural and economic heart of Southern Oregon near the California border. The largest communities in the Rogue Valley are Medford, Ashland, and Grants Pass. The most populated part of the Rogue Valley is not along the Rogue proper, but along the smaller Bear Creek tributary."*

- The Rogue River in southwestern Oregon is about 200 miles long. It flows west and southwest into the Pacific Ocean and passes through Crater Lake National Park.

The word "retreat" in its name suggests a quiet or secluded place in which one can rest and relax. Rogue people often welcome a "retreat" and a chance to get away from their current situation of being hyper-alert all the time and under constant stress.

Rogue Retreat was officially incorporated as a non-profit corporation in Oregon in 1998 and approved by the Internal Revenue Service (IRS) with 501.c.3. status in 2000.

Starting out with little money, the first official paid employee was not hired until April 1, 2009.

Rogue Retreat helped create recovery houses from 1999 to 2006. With no paid staff the organization learned many great lessons on what to do from making mistakes on what not to do. Each lesson became very valuable as the organization grew and went from five men in their first house to over 400 a night at this printing in various Rogue Retreat programs.

In 2006, Rogue Retreat shifted from running recovery houses to apartments. The program also labelled itself a homeless program rather than a recovery program and community support grew.

In 2009, two large Oregon State grants were given to Rogue Retreat to purchase its Riverside apartments and totally remodel them and to add eight apartments on South Grape Street. Part of the grant included two years of rent subsidy for those who lived in the apartments and two years of supportive services funding to pay for case managers. This put Rogue Retreat on the map.

In 2010, the State returned and partnered Rogue Retreat with the Housing Authority of Jackson County to purchase 23 more apartments and run Rogue Retreat's supportive services program through them.

Around 2014, Rogue Retreat's staff took a road trip to Portland, Oregon, to tour the Central City Concern, an organization that started in the '70s in order to help those caught in addiction. They began a sobering center on the fifth floor of a downtown building in Portland. It began small. Then, over time, the organization began to expand throughout the city.

To this day, there are over 3,000 housing opportunities such as apartments. They have a job training program, a detox center, medical clinics, and extensive staff.

It was impressive that this successful program was based on "best practices," the best way to do things that have been worked out through trial and error.

One example of a "best practice" they discovered is called "lived experience." It is the first-hand experience with mental health or substance use challenges. The word "lived" is used to differentiate between other people who have not personally lived through homelessness. A third of the organization's employees had "lived experience." They were participants at one point or another.

Often, clients begin in the detox center and then moved their way up to ultimately become staff members who happen to be very passionate about the organization and its sustainability.

Rogue Retreat adopted this policy. At the time of this writing, approximately one-third of Rogue Retreat's staff are previous participants and most all have lived experience.

In this book, you will meet two staff with "lived experience" -- Shannon and Donnie -- who were themselves homeless living on the streets. You will hear their amazing stories!

Program & Participants

In the Central City Concern program, clients were referred to as "participants" rather than clients since theirs was a "program." Rent was not charged, but rather, a "program fee" was. There needed to be some sort of monetary participation, so they tagged program agreements onto all the leases.

The reason for this is, if participants are in a program, and the people joining are not willing to follow the program rules (if, for example, they set up a meth lab in their kitchen), these individuals can be taken out of the program within 24 hours. These precautions are taken for the safety of all individuals involved.

Faith

Although Rogue Retreat is not a faith-based organization, faith is nevertheless an important aspect of its work. Faith is complete trust or confidence in someone or something. Faith has always played a key role in its growth, right from its start.

For example, one of Rogue Retreat's very first donation checks came from Kathy Bryan of the Gordon Elwood Foundation for $10,000. This check was truly a gift, as it had not been asked for. However, it was needed to help make Rogue Retreat financially stable at that point.

Some of the early foundations which chose to partner with Rogue Retreat and donate money were the Carpenter Foundation and the Oregon Community Foundation. Their support helped Rogue Retreat become the organization it is today.

These donations could be considered "acts of faith" because they were unexpected blessings that came from a "higher power" or higher source of energy in which people can invest their faith.

Most people within Rogue Retreat (staff and participants) have experienced their own faith journeys. As a result, many believe in a higher power of some kind.

Potential Partners

Rogue Retreat leaders aspire to be on the same playing field as other non-profit organizations with a 501.c.3. status with the IRS. Rogue Retreat views other non-profits as potential partners. *"If we succeed, then they succeed,"* says Chad McComas. *"We're not competing with ACCESS. We're not competing with the Housing Authority. We love them all. They need to be in this community. I think the road has been paved for us along the way to build strong partnerships."*

A prime example of this happened a few years ago. The City of Medford was giving away their fire station on West 8th Street. It was up for a competitive bid. Rogue Retreat and the Youth 71Five both put in bids for it. The council ended up choosing Youth 71Five.

Rather than becoming frustrated or disappointed their opponents had been chosen over them, Rogue Retreat (specifically, Chad) was happy for them. Another competing organization, however, became angry that they had not been chosen. They stormed out of the room.

Chad's theory is that, instead of getting upset over the successes of others, celebrate with them. You never know when they'll be potential partners.

Chapter Summary

Here are some of the key takeaways from Chapter Four:

- Rogue Retreat faced many challenges that shaped its true character in trying to meet unhoused community neighbors where they're at. The first 10 years of operations, it was run by volunteers.

- One example of a "best practice" that Rogue Retreat adopted is called "lived experience." It is first-hand experience with mental health or substance use challenges. The word "lived" is used to differentiate between other people who have not personally lived through homelessness. More than one third of the organization's employees have "lived experience."

- Although Rogue Retreat is not a faith-based organization, faith is nevertheless an important aspect of its work. Faith has always played a key role in its growth, right from its start.

- Rogue Retreat leadership aspires to be on the same playing field as other non-profit organizations with a 501.c.3. status with the IRS. Everyone else within the non-profit world is viewed as a potential partner.

In the next chapter, you will meet Shannon and Donnie, two of Rogue Retreat's staff with "lived experience."

CHAPTER FIVE:

Success Stories
(Staff with Lived Experience)

Over the years at Rogue Retreat, there have been many success stories that have captured our hearts. In this chapter, you will hear two heart-warming stories: Shannon and Donnie.

Shannon

Shannon is one of the many success stories at Rogue Retreat. At the time of this writing, she is the manager of the Kelly Shelter.

Initially, Shannon was part of Rogue Retreat in one of their apartments. Unfortunately, it didn't end well, and Shannon had to go, but no bridge was burned. She was welcome to come back when the opportunity arose. Shannon had struggled for years with a major addiction problem. Years later, she came back to Rogue Retreat and was welcomed into Hope Village with her significant other.

While at Hope Village she learned from the case management program better ways to live. She was making great progress, but still struggled with her addiction to marijuana. She ended up moving out of Hope Village to deal with life challenges on her own.

Eventually, Shannon and her significant other stopped smoking marijuana altogether. They started saving money, got jobs and were doing great. Shannon ended up applying to work at Rogue Retreat and started working at the Kelly Shelter where she is the manager today. Not only did she get a full-time job, but she also bought a house with her partner. So now, she has left the past behind her and can take care of herself again.

In the not-so-distant past, though, Shannon was homeless and a drug user. She would also hop from house to house and steal anything she could get her hands on.

Life was very challenging for her. The last few years that she was on the streets, she was on the Bear Creek Greenway with her significant other, whom she had met in a drug house. They got dumped in the middle of town by some friends and did not have anywhere else to go. She did not have any reliable family members on whom she could call.

So, Shannon decided to set up camp and stay in the middle of nowhere for about a year and a half. During that time, she and her significant other still did drugs and got into many arguments. She felt that her life was completely miserable; she did not know when she would have her next meal or how she could get warm from the cold. They were camping out, so they did not know whether people would come and rob them or if the police would come to hassle them. Life was overall rather difficult, but they tried their best to make it through.

There were times during which Shannon thought about giving up. Every time she felt like giving up, she would think, *"Well, I need to go speak to Pastor Chad."* She had known Chad for a long time from when she had been through a Rogue Retreat program once before. She believed that he could provide her with some good insight and direct her toward the path that she needed to take. She may not have done exactly what he would suggest, but it would at least get her to think.

One day, her fiancé decided to get a job. Four days clean of drugs, he got a job. Then, she and her fiancé got a vehicle, and they moved into their truck. She got back into Hope Village and eventually ended up quitting drugs, marijuana, alcohol, and cigarettes.

That is where their story of recovery began, but they chose not to stay there since they were fresh in recovery and feeling very angry. They felt frustrated and overwhelmed, so they got a sponsor and enrolled in Alcoholics Anonymous (AA).

Shannon ended up leaving Hope Village after a couple of months and moved back into her truck. But the entire time, she stayed clean, sober, and with AA. She also stayed in contact with Rogue Retreat, although she did not imagine that she would go back into their programs.

Since Shannon knew that Rogue Retreat always gave second and third chances, however, she did not give up on it so easily. No matter how far down the wrong path she had gone, she would always know that she could go back to Pastor Chad because she knew that he would provide strong insight and advice that others could not.

Shannon and her partner used to beat each other, but one day, they decided that they should love one another, that that was not the life that they ought to be living, and that they deserved much better. They wanted to be together forever, but in order to do that, they had to get their lives back on track.

Shannon claims that she would have had a hard time going on without her partner if they hadn't resolved their current situation.

She also felt that she needed to be in a relationship with her children, now that she had a grandchild. She decided to lead and choose a much different life.

Many individuals on the Greenway were single. Shannon was one of the few in a relationship. This made her unique. Many challenges came along with this, as well as transitioning from "the old life" to "the new life."

Shannon added, *"You know what, I feel like I was extremely lucky. I didn't have a lot of challenges that singles face. We've been together for six years off and on, and so during that time, we went through our own unique challenges including trying to make it in California."*

They had many challenges as a couple. Every so often, they would take it out on each other and start yelling at one another, but it was nothing like it was before their new lives.

They enrolled in the AA program and had sponsors. Things were falling into place much more smoothly than before. If Shannon or her partner were frustrated, they then had an outlet through an AA workbook or assignment.

Although Shannon was a drug addict and not an alcoholic, she and her partner both still decided to join AA because alcoholism was similar to drug addiction. She became afraid that if she went into any drug addiction recovery programs and had a bad day, she would meet one of her old drug dealers and be off and running again. It was always in the back of her mind, so AA truly helped her to change her ways, especially during the challenges she faced with her partner.

She would have other people to talk with as well. She developed a "support system" for herself. Everyone she had in her life at the time, other than the people she worked with, was clean and sober, which was a conscious choice that she had made. "Staying clean" then became mandatory in her home.

Shannon spoke of her passion for Rogue Retreat, stating it not only houses people, but also gives them the tools they need to get them out of their dire situations, such as getting driver's licences as well as help getting back on their feet again, such as finding a job.

Rogue Retreat, to Shannon, was not just a place to get a bed and some food. It was so much more, and just having that represented hope. If nothing else would be gained, then at least a better outlook would be.

Shannon has seen many people come in and out of the program, and every time she does, a small change or spark would occur, and that was the hope that would be offered. She likes to be there to encourage others, to help them know that they are worthy of a better life. It does give them hope because there have been quite a few successes, perhaps not with everyone all the time. But in her eyes, even a few successes would be worth a lot.

Thank you, Shannon, for sharing your story and for all you do!

Donnie

Donnie got clean on June 11, 2019. He had already been in the Addictions Recovery Center, Inc. (ARC) program when he heard about Rogue Retreat but didn't know much about it. When it was time for him to graduate from ARC, he was given the opportunity to join a Rogue Retreat program straight from treatment.

Since Donnie came into Rogue Retreat, he could become a productive member of society. He was in a program for about four months. Then he got the opportunity to work at Rogue Retreat, to see first-hand just how it was changing people's lives.

Donnie kept to a schedule, maintained group meetings, as well as participated in case management. Before Rogue Retreat began for him, his life was fairly chaotic. Since he became part of the program, his life has changed tremendously.

It taught him a lot of life lessons, such as how to be an independent man, which he had forgotten how to be when he was living in a society in his addiction.

Donnie said, regarding his addiction, *"My addiction was just complete insanity. You know I started getting loaded at the age of 15. My addiction really took off around 2000 right before my daughter was born."*

He added, *"Before she was born, I guess you would say I was a 'functioning addict.' I would hold down a job. I would go to work. I would still be loaded, but I would still show up."*

After his daughter was born, he started to become a bit more reckless. The drugs affected his mood, especially his attitude, so he was very unpleasant to be around. At one point, he ended up losing his job because he got into a physical altercation with someone at work. He said he was simply not himself.

His addiction took him to a very dark place. Donnie had been arrested multiple times. He took two trips to prison, and all it did was fuel his addiction further. You see, while he was in prison, he did not take advantage of what they had to offer inside. He used it more as an opportunity to become a better criminal because when he was released, he went right back to doing the same things that he was doing before.

Donnie started off living in a very nice place, but by the last blow of his addiction, he was living on the Bear Creek Greenway, in which his nights consisted of running up and down the bike path with no destination or anything worthy in sight.

The day that Donnie was "saved" by one of his closest friends was the day that he was contemplating whether he should live or die. He had finally reached the point where he didn't know what life was worth anymore. To him, it was just a bunch of meaningless acts, and he had mostly pushed away his entire family and children.

According to Donnie, his addiction destroyed every relationship that he had. But through Rogue Retreat and working through a program, he was able to restore many of his relationships. Some are still in the process of being fixed and will take a lot of time to heal. But today, he feels grateful for his recovery.

He got a job at the Kelly Shelter. Donnie would come to work and be forced to interact with others. That gave him the opportunity to be a bit more social, which was one of his greatest challenges.

Donnie has had many accomplishments that he feels proud of, but one especially poignant one is that he has been with Rogue Retreat for over two years at the time of this publication. That is the longest he has worked in one place in almost 20 years.

He typically would not stay at jobs for very long periods, so it was a huge accomplishment for him to show up every day and to be part of a program that saves people's lives every day.

He sincerely believes that if one wants to be part of the program and to work on himself or herself strongly enough, then the possibilities are endless.

In fact, it was Donnie who brought forth the idea for the book you are reading. Thank you, Donnie!

Chapter Summary

Here are some of the key takeaways from this chapter:

- Shannon and Donnie are two examples of the hundreds who've entered a door of Rogue Retreat homeless and walked out another as a valued staff member with "lived experience." Approximately one-third of Rogue Retreat's staff were previous participants.

- Rogue Retreat, to Shannon, was not just a place to get a bed and some food. It was so much more, and just having that represented hope. Shannon has seen many people come in and out of the program, and every time she does, a small change or spark would occur, and that was the hope that would be offered.

- According to Donnie, his addiction destroyed every relationship that he had. But through Rogue Retreat, and working through a program, he was able to restore many of his relationships. Some are still in the process of being fixed and will take a lot of time to heal. But today, he feels grateful for his recovery.

In the next chapter, you will learn why Rogue Retreat's case management is its "secret sauce."

The Rogue Retreat Story

CHAPTER SIX

"Secret Sauce" (Case Management)

Rogue Retreat's case management started in 1999. In recovery houses, the staff was used for light case management.

People in recovery often do not have the resources to pay for their rent. They, however, do make promises that they frequently cannot keep regarding their rent, which is one of the main reasons why the organization ended up so deeply in debt in the early years. And it is why Rogue Retreat got out of the recovery house work in 2006.

In 2015 Rogue Retreat decided to take over Heather's Haven, a recovery house founded by Max and Betty Fredericks.

When Heather's Haven was added to Rogue Retreat's program, Jackson Care Connect, a Coordinated Care Organization in Jackson County, agreed paying rent for people in recovery is well worth it in the long run as long as ladies are coming out of in-house recovery programs in better shape and recovered than they were when they went in.

"If you let them back on the streets, they're going to relapse, and you're going to lose everything you just invested." Per person, Jackson Care Connect pays $350 per month, and each resident pays around $300 per month. Several foundations also provided additional grants.

After the launch of Heather's Haven, Heather Hassett, Rogue Retreat's first paid employee, discovered a useful tool to help with case management called the "Self-Sufficiency Matrix." It possesses five levels that evaluate life skill domains like education, housing, employment, transportation, etc. based upon a 5-level scoring system. A person can be assessed on a scale of 1 to 5 depending on his or her rating in each domain.

For a homeless person, achieving life goals such as obtaining a high school diploma, getting back with family, getting kids back, and so on, are all part of each participant's unique Self-Sufficiency Matrix and case management plan.

After every six months, participants are re-assessed. Often, their scores change.

Life skills is a weekly gathering of Rogue Retreat participants where they share and celebrate successes. Guest speakers from other local organizations share what resources they have and inspire Rogue Retreat participants to take on new challenges and rise to new accomplishments.

People who enter Rogue Retreat are taught that they can do all that they want in life. Some may wish to someday start their own business or own their own homes, work full-time, even if he or she only has a high school diploma, to begin with.

Rogue Retreat invites participants to not settle for less, but rather to chase after one's dreams and not settle for things like poverty or to be stricken with a poverty-level mindset.

Case management is at the core of helping reach individuals where they are at and helping them progress along the pathway to self-sufficiency.

At one time, Rogue Retreat rented one of its buildings from Floyd Harmon. Floyd was the Executive Director of the Asante Foundation. At a meeting one day, Floyd sat down with leadership and said: *"You're not in the housing business. You're in the case management business. That's what makes you unique. You know, nobody wants to donate to you because you have apartments. They want to donate to you because you're changing lives, that's your 'secret sauce.'"*

The term stuck!

Floyd coining the phrase "secret sauce" meant that the organization had discovered the secret of case management and self-sufficiency along the way. But instead of keeping the secret recipe to themselves alone, the more that they shared the "secret sauce" with others and the more that they adapted, changed, grew, redesigned, and refined it, the greater the results.

Shannon also spoke about her experience of the "secret sauce." One of her co-workers was at Hope Village when she got there. She got her driver's licence. She expressed interest in disability insurance and started applying for food stamps. The job that she had was the first one that she had gotten in over a year. It may have been a small step for most, but to her, it was an enormous feat. No matter how small the accomplishment, she would celebrate it!

Shannon loved the "secret sauce" because it was not overwhelming to her or most people. Rather than overwhelm people with a large number of big tasks like getting a college degree, they are invited to take small steps in stages. She enjoyed how, at Rogue Retreat, accomplishments can happen so quickly and how she grew quickly from the bottom up.

In fact, at the Kelly Shelter, many successes happen daily. Shannon celebrates with the other individuals who are staying clean and sober.

"Staying here (at the Kelly Shelter) was a huge feat for this one participant," adds Shannon. *"She came from the Campground, and she has some mental issues. It's so hard for her be around all these people in a dorm-like setting with possibly 63 other individuals plus staff, plus rules. Even with all of this, she's still here."*

Shannon also spoke about some of the initial barriers that she personally encountered. For her, one of them was also being around people. Since she was on the Greenway, no one was typically around her except for herself. So when she got her vehicle, she felt as though she was thrown back into society, and it was frightening for her because she then had to be around people in order to take a shower or get food, which she found to be challenging.

At Hope Village especially, there were other people around as well as different personalities. She got into many arguments. However, because she found this unique opportunity at Rogue Retreat, she became much more motivated to have the right attitude as well as to quit drugs.

Shannon then had to deal with her emotions more directly, which she was not too fond of. To overcome this particular barrier, she moved out. She became afraid that if she would have stayed any longer at Hope Village, she would have had the police called on her.

She'd sit on the steps, read the Bible, and do her AA steps while her fiancé was working. Then after that, she began to volunteer at St. Vincent DePaul.

When she began at St. Vincent, she told the staff, *"Look, I'm not good around people, so I need to be kept upstairs. I will rearrange your upstairs. I will ball up your socks. I will fold the towels. I don't care what."*

She did this for around six or seven months when she gradually started to get comfortable being around people. Before she knew it, she was running the laundry and shower facility.

Now, a lot of the guests have her phone number because they don't have a direct line to the shelter. Shannon is a huge advocate of showing support like this, particularly at AA meetings. Having the participants know that they are cared for rather than just having volunteers or employees there for a pay check is huge for Shannon because she knows its significance and impact.

One accomplishment that Shannon said that she is most proud of is her life journey. Although she has struggled with many things throughout her life, it has all brought her to where she is today.

She's bought a new house, and it's all part of her "secret sauce" story. Despite all the bad times, she feels that nothing has ever been done in vain. Shannon is proud of the shelter and where Rogue Retreat is headed.

Donnie also had first-hand experience with the "secret sauce" case management program. He spent 25 years in addiction and got clean in June 2019. He believed that since Rogue Retreat's mission is to create opportunities for the homeless to have hope, plenty of opportunities would be made available to him if he just applied himself and participated. He regained a great deal of hope because before, as he said, he thought that his life was going to either end or that he would end up in prison.

Today, Donnie holds down a full-time job and supports others in need. He feels filled with hope in ways that he had not before, and that makes him feel truly fulfilled.

Donnie was unsure of what he was getting himself into with case management. He initially thought that Rogue Retreat was just a roof over his head and that he would simply need to touch base with his case manager every so often.

During the first meeting, his case manager Harold Nelson laid out a strategic plan of a lot of things that he would like to see Donnie accomplish by the next time he came in. If Harold had not laid out these things or used them as stepping stones, then Donnie likely wouldn't have thought of addressing half of the issues that he needed to.

For example, there were financial issues and family relationship issues. Donnie dove right in and asserted himself a bit more. Within a short period, he accomplished the goals fairly quickly because he knew that if he became stagnant in some way, he could potentially go backward.

Case management, for Donnie, was the "secret sauce" because it helped him to figure out things in his personal life that he wanted to fix. This also allowed him to become vulnerable with others. When he got into the program and met Harold, he felt safe and comfortable in ways that he could not around anyone else.

He describes the case management as the "meat and potatoes" of the program.

Donnie accomplished many goals that he never even imagined before entering the program. Since he graduated from the ARC, he began working a full-time job. He started off at Harry & David for about four months. Then, a job opened up at Rogue Retreat. He worked both jobs for about a month so that he could leave on good terms with Harry & David.

Early on, Donnie preferred to isolate himself rather than reach out to others. He was the type of person who only liked to work and have a home life. He had trouble with feeling comfortable with anyone besides his case manager, so he truly had to work on stepping outside of his comfort zone.

Heather Hassett describes the "secret sauce" as *"a progressive case management model where one level builds on another. The easiest way for me to explain it is to say that I 'reverse engineer' things in my mind. You can't do this one thing until you accomplish that thing. You can't do that until you accomplish this other thing. Working backward from the end means, for example, that we want people to increase their income and get a job."*

She believes that it is of paramount importance for participants in the program to have their immediate needs taken care of first and foremost, such as addressing mental and addiction issues. The Oregon Health Plan greatly benefits many participants, as does helping secure IDs and birth certificates. In addition, participants need to be in a safe environment of some kind.

When participants enter the Kelly Shelter or the Urban Campground or they get an apartment that they pay for on their own that is affordable, they begin to become independent and self-sufficient.

The five different levels that Heather spoke about are:

1. Immediate Needs (Level One)
2. Foundational Needs (Level Two)
3. Skill Building (Level Three)
4. Financial Literacy (Level Four)
5. Preparing to Move On (Level Five)

Heather described these five levels as the steps or levels of the "Self-Sufficiency Outcomes Matrix," which is assessed every several months or so. Participants are able to monitor growth and determine the skill levels that they are attempting to achieve.

Ultimately, their success rates are reported. Positive exits include reuniting with family, moving in with family on a permanent basis, going into drug treatment, buying a house, and so on.

Heather ultimately believes that the reason that case management works so well at Rogue Retreat is that it is intentional, client-centered. It ultimately focuses on participants' own individual goals and objectives. A great deal of encouragement is provided. At times, it seems as though the staff believes in the clients more than they believe in themselves, at least at the start.

Heather also appreciates that each case manager brings to the job his or her own experiences, background, and knowledge of different resources.

For more information, visit rogueretreat.org/supportive-services.

Chapter Summary

Here are some key takeaways from this chapter:

- For an addict or homeless person, achieving life goals such as obtaining a high school diploma, getting back with family, getting kids back, and so on, are all part of each participant's unique case management plan.

- Rogue Retreat invites participants to not settle for less, but rather to chase after one's dreams and not settle for things like poverty or to be stricken with a poverty-level mindset.

- Shannon has many pieces of advice to give those who are entering the Kelly Shelter for the first time. She said to keep an open mind, to keep the lines of communication open, and to keep the doors open.

- At a meeting one day, Floyd Harmon sat down with leadership and said, *"You're not in the housing business. You're in the case management business. That's what makes you unique. You know, nobody wants to donate to you because you have apartments. They want to donate to you because you're changing lives, that's your 'secret sauce.'"* The term stuck!

- Donnie also had firsthand experience with the "secret sauce" case management program. He spent 25 years in addiction and got clean in June 2019. He believed that since Rogue Retreat's mission is to create opportunities for the homeless to have hope, plenty of opportunities would be made available to him if he just applied himself and participated. He regained a great deal of hope because before, as he said, he thought that his life was going to either end or that he would end up in prison. Today, Donnie holds down a full-time job and supports others in need. He feels filled with hope in ways that he had not before, and that makes him feel truly fulfilled.

In the next chapter, you will learn about three model programs: Hope Village, Kelly Shelter, and the Medford Urban Campground.

CHAPTER SEVEN

Hope Village, Kelly Shelter, Medford Urban Campground

(Three Program Models)

Rogue Retreat currently offers multiple tiers of housing programs serving 400+ participants under its roof every night.

In this chapter, you will discover stories behind three model programs that are examples of the first three of six tiers:

- transitional housing (Hope Village),
- transitional shelter (Kelly Shelter), and
- transitional camping (Medford Urban Campground).

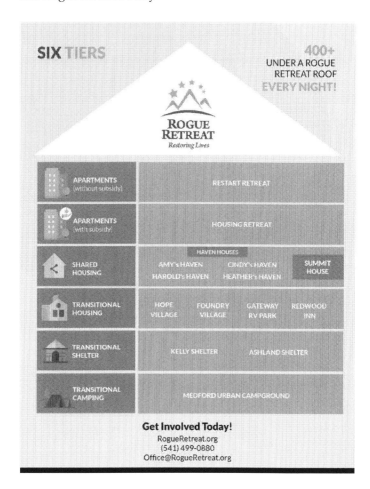

Model Program: Hope Village

A woman recently got admitted to Hope Village who had come from an Oxford House. She didn't have a job that paid enough to rent a bedroom in an Oxford House, but she wanted to stay clean and sober.

She was admitted into Hope Village, where she started out with $85 per month as her program fee. She said, *"I'm just happy to be here. I feel safe here. I look forward to putting my life back together. You folks here are awesome. Your staff is awesome."*

Although tiny houses are not the most glamorous homes, each is nevertheless offered as a safe space for a participant to stay, which is a big step in the right direction for many.

Chad is excited to take people on tours, to show them Hope Village is a dignified place to live where people have more independence. There are a few minor rules to follow. He believes homeless individuals are finally regaining their dignity, especially since they can shower, wash, have their own mailbox, do their own laundry, and so on.

As participants leave the village each day, they look like any other citizen in the community. They have jobs, they get involved with organizations, and they volunteer and associate like anyone else. The amount of dignity they gain from being in Hope Village is enormous.

Hope Village was a dream of Rogue Retreat, St. Vincent DePaul, and the Jackson County Homeless Taskforce. In 2014 they began researching, gathering data and visiting other villages in Oregon to find creative ways to serve the homeless in Jackson County. The first tiny house community in Southern Oregon, Hope Village opened its doors on October 31, 2017. To date more than 300 participants have gone through the Hope Village program since it opened.

Hope Village is a transitional supportive housing program for homeless men, women, and couples in a community setting of attractive, well-designed, and insulated tiny house duplex units and shared facilities. Shared facilities include a commercial kitchen, restrooms, showers, a laundry room, a community center, a park area, a dog park and a vegetable garden.

The village is safe, sanitary, gated, and supervised by on-site staff. Daily village chores and weekly house inspections teach villagers how to care for their living unit and become good future tenants and good neighbors.

Village participants are required to meet weekly with their case managers to help empower them to break the cycle of poverty and homelessness. They help them work on permanent ways to get off the streets, address their individual barriers, and transition back into society.

Case managers assist villagers to identify short-term and long-term goals, obtain vital identification documents, sign up for food assistance, health insurance and seek medical, mental health, or substance use treatment when and if necessary. Participants complete or further their education, seek employment or other stable sources of income, address any legal issues and find a more permanent housing solution.

55% of Hope Village participants transition to more permanent housing. For some, that is residential treatment or reuniting with family. For some, it is moving up to a Rogue Retreat apartment or available community rental. Indeed, Rogue Retreat restores lives.

Check out Hope Village:

rogueretreat.org/housing-shelter

Model Program: Kelly Shelter

When asked about the Kelly Shelter and what it entails, Shannon, shelter manager, states it is a homeless shelter for those who choose to stay. People are permitted to "try out" the shelter for seven days without any strings attached. They dry out, get warm, get a shower and get some food.

If people want to stay for up to six months, the Kelly Shelter offers case management to help them obtain a driver's licence, food stamps, health insurance, and more. Peer Support Specialists are available to talk to participants when they're needed. They're available for any type of problem such as feelings of being overwhelmed.

The Kelly Shelter, in Shannon's words, is essentially a place where one can "call home" for six months, and then all efforts are put forth to transition the participant into more stable housing. Shannon appreciates and enjoys her experience at Rogue Retreat (especially the Kelly Shelter). She highly recommends it for anyone who is homeless or is in need.

As for the Kelly Shelter, there have been many individuals who have been chronically homeless who have said: *"I've been to a lot of shelters, but this is the best one."* Some of the aspects of the Kelly Shelter that make it so strong are the caring staff, reasonable rules, tasty food, the ability to have a hot shower, clean clothes and case managers who are willing to work with each person on his or her personal needs.

Through a partnership with ACCESS, Rogue Retreat has expanded the Kelly Shelter into a 64-bed facility that opened year-round on November 21, 2019. The Kelly Shelter is now the first year-round, low barrier (housing first) shelter in Southern Oregon.

Shannon has many pieces of advice to give those who are entering the Kelly Shelter for the first time. She said to keep an open mind, to keep the lines of communication open, and to keep the doors open.

If Donnie had to give anyone advice who was looking to enter the Kelly Shelter, he would tell them they need to forget what they thought they know and become teachable. Also, he would tell them it is important to have faith in the program itself.

According to Chad, he feels very humbled every time he walks into the facility to see the amazing staff as well as people of all ages. Many seniors are also in this particular shelter. It seems as though they should have their own little apartment, in Chad's eyes, but due to economic issues, this cannot occur at the moment. At least, he says, the older individuals are safe and won't be taken advantage of as they might be on the streets.

The Kelly Shelter is under the guidance and direction of the Kelly Shelter Steering Committee, made up of local church leaders, agencies, and concerned citizens. The daily operations are managed by the Shelter Manager under the supervision of the Rogue Retreat Operations and Supportive Services Directors. Each shift is hosted by paid, trained employees.

The Kelly Shelter is a great example of community support. Restaurants, churches and other donors buy, prepare and deliver the evening meals. Often, they donate one meal per month for 64 guests who reside in the shelter. These donations not only serve the shelter participants, but help the donors connect with the homeless population. So often eyes are opened to who makes up the homeless community and how amazing these individuals are.

Check out the Kelly Shelter:

rogueretreat.org/housing-shelter

Model Program: Medford Urban Campground

On July 2, 2020, the Medford City Council voted to approve a request from the County Sheriff and the City Police Chief to create an urban campground to help the homeless combat COVID-19 and prevent fire hazards on the Greenway in the Rogue Valley.

This was a dream of Rogue Retreat for years. They saw the need to have an entry-level campground to provide a place for the homeless in the community to be when they are exited off community sidewalks, parks and in Medford's case, the Greenway.

The site is both neat and clean, but is nevertheless still a tent on the ground. There is no heat or air conditioning. Chad will apologize to the participants stating: *"I wish we had something better for you, but this is what we got for you now."*

In return, the participants always respond, *"Hey, we're just thrilled and grateful to be here."*

Then, Chad often asks why.

"We're safe, behind the fence," they reply. *"My stuff is safe. I can leave it here, and nobody is going to steal it. I can sleep at night. I don't have to worry about being attacked and getting my stuff stolen."*

Then, they usually have a big smile on their face and say: *"Thank you for letting me be here."*

Starting with only 25 campsites, the Medford Urban Campground has expanded to 70 tent sites (Phase 1), 25 pallet shelters and 10 tiny houses (Phase 2) at the time of this writing. The City of Medford and the local community want Rogue Retreat to expand it further to up to 150 sites and move it from the original location as a temporary campground to a more permanent one.

In fact, urban campgrounds, based on the Rogue Retreat model, are being discussed in cities all over Oregon and being planned for neighboring Grants Pass and Ashland.

The Medford Urban Campground is an entry-level tent and pallet shelter, a safe haven for the homeless coming directly from the streets and referred by Medford City Police Department's Livability Team. Guests receive meals donated by community partners as well as wrap-around social services from community agencies.

Check out the Medford Urban Campground:

rogueretreat.org/housing-shelter

Chapter Summary

Here are some key takeaways from this chapter:

- Rogue Retreat currently offers at least six tiers of programs serving 400+ participants under its roof every night.

- Hope Village is Southern Oregon's first and model gated tiny house community for homeless men, women, and couples. It is an attractive, well-designed, and insulated tiny house duplex units and shared facilities. Shared facilities include a commercial kitchen, a restroom and shower facility, laundry room, a community center, a park area, a dog park and a vegetable garden. The village is safe, sanitary, gated, and supervised by on-site staff.

- The Kelly Shelter is now the first year-round, low barrier (housing first) shelter in Southern Oregon for up to 64 people sheltered per night. Shower and laundry services are available on-site.

- The Medford Urban Campground started with 25 campsites, but has expanded to 70 tent sites (Phase 1) and 25 pallet shelters and 10 tiny houses (Phase 2) with City approval. The City of Medford and the local community want Rogue Retreat to expand it from the original location approved as a temporary campground to a more permanent one. In fact, Urban Campgrounds

> based on the Rogue Retreat model are being discussed by other Oregon cities and planned for neighboring Grants Pass and Ashland.

In the next chapter, you will learn about three social enterprise models run by Rogue Retreat: Thrift Shop, Clean Sweep, and Hope University.

CHAPTER EIGHT

Thrift Shop, Clean Sweep, And Hope University

(Three Social Enterprise Models)

Social Enterprise Model: Thrift Shop

The Thrift Shop by Rogue Retreat started in 2014 to create an additional source of revenue and donations to support Rogue Retreat programs.

Thrift Shops are a great source of income for a non-profit since there is no cost for inventory. The sheer goodwill of the community is relied upon to make donations. Since most people look to donate their items somewhere, it becomes a win-win for everyone:

- People who want to get involved give out their gently-used items.
- There are good, cheap deals for those who are unable to afford regular clothing.
- It turns out to be a nice deal for both the volunteers as well as the ones who work there. Senior citizens who want to do something with their lives, volunteer. They love it. They have the chance to shop every day, feel useful, make a difference, and be happy.
- All profits support the organization's mission.

In 2012, Chad visited Father Joe's organization in San Diego, California. It is an 'amazing organization' started by Father Jo, a Catholic priest, 30-40 years ago. It started with Father Jo giving out peanut butter sandwiches to the homeless on the streets.

Now it's a $30-$40-million-a-year operation. According to their marketing department one-third of their income comes from their thrift stores. Their thrift stores sell cars, furniture, clothing, and so on. This inspired Chad and the Rogue Retreat board to start a thrift store for Rogue Retreat.

According to Chad, Rogue Retreat's Thrift Shop works to bless the larger community. It partners with other local thrift stores like Habitat for Humanity and Goodwill. Any items Rogue Retreat's thrift shop can't use are passed on.

In fact, Chad adds: "*We even give a tithing check out every month. If we make a profit, we'll send 10% to another community organization in Medford. We want them to know we're all in this together. Our success is your success. It's more than just an income stream.*"

Shopping at the Thrift Shop helps change lives, too. All proceeds from the Thrift Shop support the Homeless Supportive Housing/Shelter programs of Rogue Retreat.

The Thrift Shop also acts as a job training program for Rogue Retreat participants who require developing meaningful work experiences.

There are many opportunities to volunteer at the Thrift Shop, too. Volunteers are needed to help cashiers, accept and sort donations and set up merchandise displays.

Check out the Thrift Shop by Rogue Retreat online at:

rogueretreat.org/enterprises

Social Enterprise Model: Clean Sweep

Created as a partnership between the City of Medford and Rogue Retreat in 2018, Clean Sweep is a collaborative clean-up and job readiness program. Participants from the Kelly Shelter, Hope Village, Urban Campground and other Rogue Retreat programs develop healthy work habits and gain valuable employment experience to restore their lives while keeping our streets and community clean!

The mission of Clean Sweep is to improve the community's image of the homeless while providing work opportunities for them. Clean Sweep creates routes to clean the streets of Medford. For a couple of hours of work, our homeless volunteers get a $10 gift certificate, which is very helpful to them. They are not paid employees, but considered volunteers with a gift at the end of their shifts.

As soon as homeless volunteers put on their green vests to volunteer their time, they suddenly go from being unnoticed in the community to being highly appreciated. People begin to wave, honk their horns, drive by and yell out the window, *"Thanks so much for what you're doing."* They feel so important from all the attention that they receive.

They hope this work can lead to more work through a regular job.

The staff works closely with each worker to identify what is needed for them to move forward. It may be simple like getting their identification or a social security card. Or, it may be more involved like a resume, online job applications, and referrals.

In Chad's eyes, Clean Sweep does far more than just clean streets, which is vital in and of itself. It's good for the city, businesses, and the homeless.

In Clean Sweep's first two years:

- Over 21,000 pounds of trash were picked up.

- An average of 40-65 pounds of trash was picked up per day.

- Over 1,200 volunteer hours were donated by 172 homeless individuals.

- 22+ homeless volunteers transitioned to regular employment.

Social Enterprise Model: Hope University

Hope University, according to Chad, is ultimately *"a way to train and educate other communities. We pat them on the back, pump them up, tell them we made every mistake in the book. Learn from our mistakes so you don't have to make them. They're thrilled."*

To meet the need expressed by neighboring communities in creating, funding and operating housing and shelter programs like those offered by Rogue Retreat, Hope University was started in 2019 to educate and train leaders to bring hope, stability, and a clear path to the sufficiency for homeless in-crisis.

As proof of its experience operating programs using "best practices," Hope University tapped the expertise of Rogue Retreat staff and community partners to develop a series of 101 "best practice" teleconferences now available as 101 audio courses (for purchase): Clean Sweep 101, Community Village Creation 101, Urban Campgrounds 101 and Winter Shelters 101. Featured are multiple special guests and experienced staff.

Best practices in the first four 101 audio courses include 12.75 hours of audio training with 213 pages of transcriptions and 66 handouts. More than 30 communities to-date have purchased these 101 audio courses for their communities.

More 101 courses are being designed. Stay tuned!

Rogue Retreat Model of Success is shared with communities:

- **Shelter & Housing**: Innovative, temporary, and transitional shelter and housing with solutions that stabilize formerly homeless and give them a place to call home.
- **Supportive Services**: Rogue Retreat's "secret sauce" is a self-sufficiency framework that restores lives with guidance, counselling, and referrals to community partners who focus on overcoming barriers.
- **Community Partners**: A comprehensive network of service providers that provide wrap-around services and join with us to help participants reach their highest potential.
- **Funders**: Individuals and organizations who invest time, money, goods, and services that further our vision and mission.
- **Hope**: Lifts the broken-hearted. Sparks belief in positive outcomes. Infuses the model with goodness.

Case Study

As an example of its customized training capacity, Hope University helped the Roseburg Homeless Commission conduct a Community Needs Assessment for those who are unsheltered. The process that leads to an action plan for improving homeless safety net services in the Roseburg community began in March of 2021.

The first step included conducting a needs survey of unsheltered individuals, an online survey for community members, and zoom and phone interviews with community leaders, which is called a "listening tour." In total, over 80 members of the Roseburg community took part in the listening tour and helped draft an action plan (road map) for the community to execute.

The results were reviewed at a Strategic Visioning meeting. The action plan was presented and reviewed by the Homeless Commission and City Staff.

The resulting vision statement says, "Roseburg envisions an inclusive community where all feel safe, supported, and have the opportunity to work towards becoming self-sufficient. This will be accomplished through building a sustainable, coordinated social service-based network to address the needs of the unhoused. Lasting success will be founded on the principle of collective engagement with the entire community."

To realize this vision, the Homeless Commission will begin creating tactical sub-committees that will focus on accomplishing short-term goals first, which will lead the way to program creation. Short-term goals include:

- Create a Navigation Center. Roseburg already received funding to create the Center!
- Identify the lead organization or organizations to help stand up and operate the programs. The lead organization or organizations will have the

bottom-line responsibility of managing the day-to-day operations of the programs.

- Create a comprehensive property inventory for potential program development.
- Facilitate a forum to develop a perspective and strategy related to information sharing and referrals.
- Create an outreach and livability sub-committee of the Homeless Commission to focus just on the short-term needs of the homeless.
- Investigate potential ordinance updates to help create a pathway for program creation.

Capacity Building

Hope University builds capacity for interested communities by offering such deliverables as:

Phase I (Listening Tour)

1. Conduct homeless needs assessment

2. Compile community resource guide and identify gaps and potential partnerships

3. Provide tours of active homeless programs and services

4. Provide virtual training with Rogue Retreat staff

5. Provide technical assistance and coaching

6. Facilitate strategic visioning session

7. Create a 3-year action plan/roadmap

Phase II (Training)

1. Poverty simulation

2. Fundamentals of peer support

3. De-Escalation techniques

4. ACES and trauma-informed care

It is truly an honor to get to help other communities address the needs of their unsheltered.

Email Hope University directly at HopeU@rogueretreat.org.

Check out Hope University online at: rogueretreat.org/hope-university.

Chapter Summary

Here are some key takeaways from this chapter:

- The Thrift Shop offers a variety of items at discounted prices for the community. They accept gently-used donations to resell to the community. All proceeds support the Homeless Supportive Housing/Shelter programs of Rogue Retreat. The Thrift Shop also acts as a job training program for Rogue Retreat participants who require developing meaningful work experience.

- The mission of Clean Sweep by Rogue Retreat is to improve the community's image while providing work opportunities for our homeless volunteers. For a couple of hours of work, the homeless volunteers get a $10 gift certificate. As soon as they put on their highly visible green vests, people begin to wave, honk their horns, drive by, yell out the windows: *"Thanks so much for what you're doing."*

- In Clean Sweep's first two years, over 21,000 pounds of trash were picked up, an average of 40-65 pounds of trash were picked up per day, over 1,200 volunteer hours were donated by 172 homeless and 22+ homeless transitioned to employment.

- Hope University, according to Chad, is ultimately *"a way to train and educate other communities. We pat them on the back, pump them up, tell them we made every mistake in the book. Learn from our mistakes so you don't have to make them. They're thrilled."* There are four audio courses: Clean Sweep 101, Community Village Creation 101, Urban Campground 101, and Winter Shelters 101 (with more 101 courses in development). Hope University also helps communities like neighboring Roseburg build their capacity by conducting Listening Tours including a Community Needs Assessment for those who are unsheltered and an action plan for improving homeless safety net services.

In the next chapter, you will learn about Rogue Retreat's plans for expansion.

CHAPTER NINE

Its Expansion Plan of 'One More Bed'

There are many small steps leading to the larger goal of attempting to end homelessness altogether, such as repairing one's rental history, restoring credit rating, getting IDs, and addressing other specific needs of our homeless community.

According to Chad: *"We have to get to the place where we have enough affordable housing so that people who want to be housed have that opportunity. Housing authorities, cities, families, faith-based groups, non-profits, we are all working to add beds."*

Adding a single bed at a time may seem like a small step. But, that bed can make a huge difference for an unhoused individual. For example, anytime that a bed can be added inside a house, shelter, village, campground, community, etc., a sense of hope is instilled one more time to one more neighbor.

Along with more affordable housing, 'one more bed' may just be the mantra that ends homelessness.

Although the goal was to keep putting beds wherever they can be placed legally and safely, the ultimate objective is case management and to prepare participants for permanent housing, even if that means starting in a tent in the urban campground. Participants learn how to live in a community.

Then, they might move into a shelter from the campground. They learn how to better work and thrive in a community, learn how to take care of themselves, get a job, move into a tiny house at Hope Village or a studio apartment. They go out into the marketplace and look to rent a place somewhere.

Community leaders are also beginning to awaken and say: *"We need to do something in our community."* Some are even inspired to make a bold declaration to end homelessness by the year 2030.

The Medford city council voted in 2021 to clean up Bear Creek Greenway, but they became aware that they not only had to clean the Greenway itself, but start to figure out where exactly to place the homeless who are displaced.

It appears that a significant number of community leaders are willing to take on more responsibility and commit to more creative projects than even four or five years ago.

There are misunderstandings of the homeless in every community, but the leadership of Rogue Retreat has been able to move past these and to break down barriers including NIMBY's, people who may want shelters, but just 'not in my back yard'.

The key to changing community perception is educating the public and businesses at every corner while embracing windows of opportunity that open up. Making one right decision after another has served to solidify Rogue Retreat as an organization that brings hope to the hopeless.

Rogue Retreat has figured out if everyone works the 'secret sauce' and does a better job extending a hand to help people out of the well of homelessness, to help them get their lives back and do that well, we will enjoy many more opportunities to add one more bed here and another bed there.

Rogue Retreat staff, board and supporters are humbled to be part of the solution to end homelessness!

Thank you, too, for the part that you play, whatever that might be!

Chapter Summary

Here are some key takeaways from this chapter:

- Adding a single bed at a time may seem like a small step. But, that bed can make a huge difference for an unhoused individual. For example, anytime that a bed can be added inside a house, shelter, village, campground, community, etc., a sense of hope is instilled one more time to one more homeless individual.

- Along with more affordable housing, 'one more bed' may just be the mantra that ends homelessness.

- Rogue Retreat has figured out that if everyone works the 'secret sauce' and does a better job extending a hand to help people out of the well of homelessness, to help them get their lives back and do that well, we will enjoy many more opportunities to add one more bed here and another bed there.

In the next chapter, you will learn four ways that you can get involved...

CHAPTER TEN

Four Ways to Get Involved

#1 Sign Up for a Tour

There are many benefits to getting a tour at Rogue Retreat. Here are three:

First, it is a very minimal investment of time. But, there is a very high return on investment of your time.

Second, tours ultimately change perceptions and points of view. On one tour, Chad was standing by the entrance to the urban campground with the people on the tour and he asked: *"What do you see?"*

The initial reaction of the people was it was "clean" and "neat." Then Chad proceeded to say, *"So what were your perceptions about a campground before you saw it? You thought it would be dirty, right? You thought it would just be junky and terrible?"* They said *"yes".*

"But now that you see it, it changes everything, doesn't it?"

Chad believes the general public has these same thoughts as well. Many imagine a managed campground site set up for the homeless will be trashy just like the unsanctioned ones seen around any town.

Tours change perceptions. When participants introduce themselves, they often share their stories. Hearts are typically touched on a deeper level, and those on the tours are inspired to be more supportive.

When tours were started years ago at Hope Village, whether it was individuals from the Chamber of Commerce, the bank, or the state government, attendees all said the same thing, *"This is not what we expected."*

Third, tours are vital to building an image and then that image leads to opportunities that ultimately lead to involvement like volunteering or even donating. At times, when people visit and take a tour, the next step they take is to write a check and before much time passes, they become regular donors.

People often want to volunteer to be on the various boards or steering committees of Rogue Retreat. Everyone can get involved in some way. Professional people are always needed, whether it is through giving their time, being on a board, cutting hair, serving meals, or helping to make decisions in some way.

Sign up for a tour by calling (541) 499-0880. Or, visit rogueretreat.org/tour.

#2 Volunteer

Many individuals are inspired to pursue their passions and to get involved in one way or another. One gentleman, for example, had just retired as a lawyer. He loves to help the homeless deal with situations such as helping them to get their driver's licence, dealing with felonies, and addressing legal issues they're facing.

Some of the obstacles that have become major roadblocks for the homeless are things that the volunteers enjoy assisting them with, such as helping them to figure out how to do the paperwork for being approved for disability assistance or certain life skills.

One person on a tour might make a statement such as: *"I love to cook. Can we make food for your shelter?"* A reply might be: *"Yes, every night, we need a meal for our 64 people in the Kelly Shelter."* Then they often say: *"I can do one meal a month."* They get their friends together, make a meal, bring it down, and serve it to the participants. This becomes a win/win type of situation. People can sign up for meals at various Rogue Retreat facilities on Mealtrain.com.

There are many other ways to get involved at Rogue Retreat. Sometimes hairstylists say: *"Can I give free haircuts at the Campground?"* A response might be: *"We'd love free haircuts at the Campground."* So, they would bring their friends in and cut 60 people's hair. It makes the homeless feel good about themselves, makes them look good and enables them to go job seeking.

Individuals who volunteer their time feel good about themselves because they just helped people in crisis. They didn't get paid financially for it, but they got paid in a different way.

Even if it was something as simple as filing or photocopying, there are a variety of ways to get involved. If you have a skill to offer, please let us know!

In Grants Pass, a Foundry Village Steering Committee was established. It was made up of volunteers who are leaders from the local community. This committee of volunteers helped get people involved in the operations, fundraising and construction of Foundry Village which opened the day before Thanksgiving 2021.

To volunteer, call (541) 499-0880 to ask how you can volunteer and offer your skillset. Or visit rogueretreat.org/volunteer.

#3 Get a Job at Rogue Retreat

With its rapid growth, there are many job positions at Rogue Retreat needing to be filled. This type of work may be a bit frightening to the general public, but not to the people who had been through the program already.

Many Rogue Retreat employees have had life experience of addiction, abusive relationships, dysfunctional families and more. As they have pulled themselves out of the situation and built a new foundation in their lives, they become great employees with the empathy and knowledge needed to serve the homeless population Rogue Retreat serves.

Rogue Retreat is continually looking for excellent employees to be guest hosts at shelters, campgrounds, and tiny house villages. They are able to speak to the participants in a way others can't. They can call clients out, observe patterns of behavior others cannot see, and be quite honest with the clients. The employees become inspirations to the clients they work with.

One of the difficulties of working for a non-profit agency is not making a great amount of money as one might in a commercial organization. But a core reason people love working at Rogue Retreat is that they're making a difference in the lives of others. Often employees come to work thinking to themselves: *"I'm glad to go to work today because I'm going to change lives."*

Many people dread their jobs, no matter how much money they are or are not making. For non-profit organizations like Rogue Retreat, however, employees often go home every night feeling excited that they had the chance to touch lives and to be part of an experience that matters – which, in the end, is better than money.

The process of altruism is when people know that they're making a difference in the world and begin to see how their work truly matters – no matter how seemingly insignificant or small it may seem at the time.

For career opportunities, visit rogueretreat.org/careers.

#4 Donate

In addition to donating your skills (#3), consider donating cash, basic items, and meals!

Cash

There are many opportunities to give financially to specific programs like Hope Village, Kelly Shelter, Urban Campground, Clean Sweep, etc. Some donors prefer to give monthly, like the 180 Club which asks for monthly giving starting at $25 a month.

Without supporters our work is not possible. Each night Rogue Retreat houses and shelters over 400 people.

Rogue Retreat is not called to warehouse people. Rogue Retreat is called to help people restore their lives and move forward out of homelessness.

Basic Items

You may also donate basic items. For example, shelters always welcome donations of cash, groceries, and clothes, but there are ways to customize what you give.

First, ask the shelter what they need most. Second, consider the time of the year, and donate summer clothes in the warmer months or winter clothes when it's cold. Think about donating toiletries or personal items including bras, underwear, and socks.

Meals

At places like the Kelly Shelter, Ashland Shelter, and Medford Urban Campground, you can volunteer to cook a meal for unsheltered guests. Taking the time to help prepare and serve a meal means so much to someone staying at the shelter. When you reach out with compassion and a servant's heart, you not only provide a meal but a feeling of hope during a difficult time.

Please support our services today by donating.

Call (541) 499-0880. Or visit rogueretreat.org/support.

Chapter Summary

Here are some key takeaways from this chapter:

- Tours have a very high return on investment of your time. Many imagine that urban campground sites set up for the homeless would be trashy just like the ones seen on the Bear Creek Greenway. Tours change perceptions.

- When tours were started years ago at Hope Village, whether it was individuals from the Chamber of Commerce, the bank, or the state government, attendees all said the same thing, *"This is not what we expected."*

- Many individuals are inspired to pursue their passions and to get involved in one way or another. One person might make a statement: *"I love to cook. Can we make food for your shelter?"* Sometimes hair stylists might come along and say: *"Can I give free haircuts at the Campground?"* The answer is yes.

- With its rapid growth, there are now many job positions looking to be filled at any given time.

- Some of the difficulties of working for a non-profit agency are, of course, that one will not make a great amount of money as one might in a commercial organization. But a core reason that people love working at Rogue Retreat is that they're making a difference in the lives of others.

- There are many opportunities to give financially to specific programs like Hope Village, Kelly Shelter, Urban Campground, Clean Sweep, etc. Some donors prefer to give monthly, to the 180 Club.

- Without supporters Rogue Retreat's work is not possible. Each night Rogue Retreat houses and shelters over 400 people.

Final Words

Rogue Retreat, started as a dream in 1998, has become a strong non-profit in Medford housing over 400 a night and growing to help other communities find ways to serve their own homeless communities.

Rogue Retreat has been founded on Hope and Faith. Rogue Retreat staff reaches the unsheltered where they are at and strives to give hope to the homeless and have faith that by doing the "Next Right Thing," goals will be achieved.

We have sensed a favour on our work which, we believe, comes by helping those who can't help themselves.

These are the orphans, widows, poor and strangers in the community who don't have support groups to offer the help they need. These groups have no family to fall on or look to for encouragement.

These are the homeless who fall into the "well of homelessness" and can't get out on their own. They need a hand-up (not a handout) so they can get on their feet and begin to rebuild their lives.

We have learned at Rogue Retreat that there is a wonderful sense of accomplishment by giving the hand-up and seeing at least 50% of those become self-sufficient and self-sustaining citizens of the community who in turn begin to give back and pay it forward.

The Rogue Retreat Story

References

1. 'Careers.' Rogue Retreat.
   https://www.rogueretreat.org/careers/
2. 'Corporate Giving.' Rogue Retreat.
   https://www.rogueretreat.org/giving/
3. 'Giving.' Rogue Retreat.
   https://www.rogueretreat.org/giving/
4. 'Hope Village.' Rogue Retreat.
   https://www.rogueretreat.org/housing-shelter/
5. 'Hope University.' Rogue Retreat.
   https://www.rogueretreat.org/hope-university/
6. 'Kelly Shelter.' Rogue Retreat.
   https://www.rogueretreat.org/housing-shelter/
7. 'Media Kit.' Rogue Retreat.
   https://www.rogueretreat.org/media/
8. 'Raising Hope.' Rogue Retreat.
   https://www.rogueretreat.org/campaign/
9. 'Rogue Retreat.' https://www.rogueretreat.org/
10. 'Rogue Valley.' Wikipedia. Wikimedia Foundation,
    Accessed July 8, 2021.
    https://en.wikipedia.org/wiki/Rogue_Valley
11. 'Social Enterprises.' Rogue Retreat.
    https://www.rogueretreat.org/enterprises/
12. 'Supportive Services.' Rogue Retreat.
    https://www.rogueretreat.org/supportive-services/
13. 'Take a Tour.' Rogue Retreat.
    https://www.rogueretreat.org/tour/

14. 'Thrift Shop.' Rogue Retreat.
https://www.rogueretreat.org/enterprises/
15. 'Training.' Rogue Retreat.
https://www.rogueretreat.org/training/
16. 'Volunteer.' Rogue Retreat.
https://www.rogueretreat.org/volunteer/
17. 'Ways to Give.' Rogue Retreat.
https://www.rogueretreat.org/support/

Made in the USA
Monee, IL
31 May 2022

97297113R00052